EPIC

EPIC BOOKS are no ordinary books. They burst with intense action, high-speed heroics, and shadows of the unknown. Are you ready for an Epic adventure?

This edition first published in 2026 by Bellwether Media, Inc.

No part of this publication may be reproduced in whole or in part without written permission of the publisher. For information regarding permission, write to Bellwether Media, Inc., Attention: Permissions Department, 3500 American Blvd W, Suite 150, Bloomington, MN 55431.

Library of Congress Cataloging-in-Publication Data

LC record for Invisibility available at: https://lccn.loc.gov/2025021831

Text copyright © 2026 by Bellwether Media, Inc. EPIC and associated logos are trademarks and/or registered trademarks of Bellwether Media, Inc. Bellwether Media is a division of FlutterBee Education Group.

Editor: Rachael Barnes   Designer: Gabriel Hilger

Printed in the United States of America, North Mankato, MN.

TABLE OF CONTENTS

HIDDEN IN PLAIN SIGHT ………. 4

CURLED AROUND CORAL …… 6

MOVING MOSS ………………… 10

FOREST FEATHERS …………… 14

HOPPING HIDERS …………… 18

GLOSSARY ……………………… 22

TO LEARN MORE ……………… 23

INDEX …………………………… 24

HIDDEN IN PLAIN SIGHT

Some animals can blend into their surroundings. No one can spot them! They become **invisible**.

Animals might blend in to surprise their **prey**. Hidden animals are also safe from attacks.

CURLED AROUND CORAL

SNACK SIZED
Many pygmy sea horses are less than 1 inch (2.5 centimeters) long!

Pygmy sea horses are hard to spot. They are some of the world's smallest sea horses.

To other fish, sea horses make an easy meal. Sea horses must stay hidden to stay alive.

BARGIBANT'S PYGMY SEA HORSE

CLASS: FISH

LIFE SPAN: UNKNOWN

STATUS IN THE WILD

| LEAST CONCERN | NEAR THREATENED | VULNERABLE | ENDANGERED | CRITICALLY ENDANGERED | EXTINCT IN THE WILD | EXTINCT |

RANGE

Pygmy sea horses live in **coral reefs**. Their bodies match the colors and **textures** of their coral home.

CORAL REEF

TAIL

PREY

Pygmy sea horses curl their tails around coral. They **camouflage** themselves. They can surprise their prey!

MOVING MOSS

Is it moss or a frog? It is tough to tell! Mossy frogs have green bodies with dark spots. They are bumpy to touch.

They look like moss. Even their eyes blend into their surroundings!

VIETNAMESE MOSSY FROG

CLASS: AMPHIBIAN

LIFE SPAN: AROUND 10 YEARS

STATUS IN THE WILD

| LEAST CONCERN | NEAR THREATENED | VULNERABLE | ENDANGERED | CRITICALLY ENDANGERED | EXTINCT IN THE WILD | EXTINCT |

RANGE

11

Mossy frogs live in **rain forests** near water. They are active at night.

RAIN FOREST

HERE OR THERE?

Vietnamese mossy frogs can "throw" their voice. They can make their voice sound up to 13 feet (4 meters) away!

While sleeping, they flatten out to hide. If scared, mossy frogs curl up to look smaller. **Predators** pass them by.

FOREST FEATHERS

Eastern screech owls are small. They only grow up to 10 inches (25 centimeters) tall!

During the day, eastern screech owls are often tucked away in tree holes. Their size helps keep them hidden.

EASTERN SCREECH OWL

CLASS: BIRD

LIFE SPAN: UP TO 14 YEARS

STATUS IN THE WILD

| LEAST CONCERN | NEAR THREATENED | VULNERABLE | ENDANGERED | CRITICALLY ENDANGERED | EXTINCT IN THE WILD | EXTINCT |

RANGE

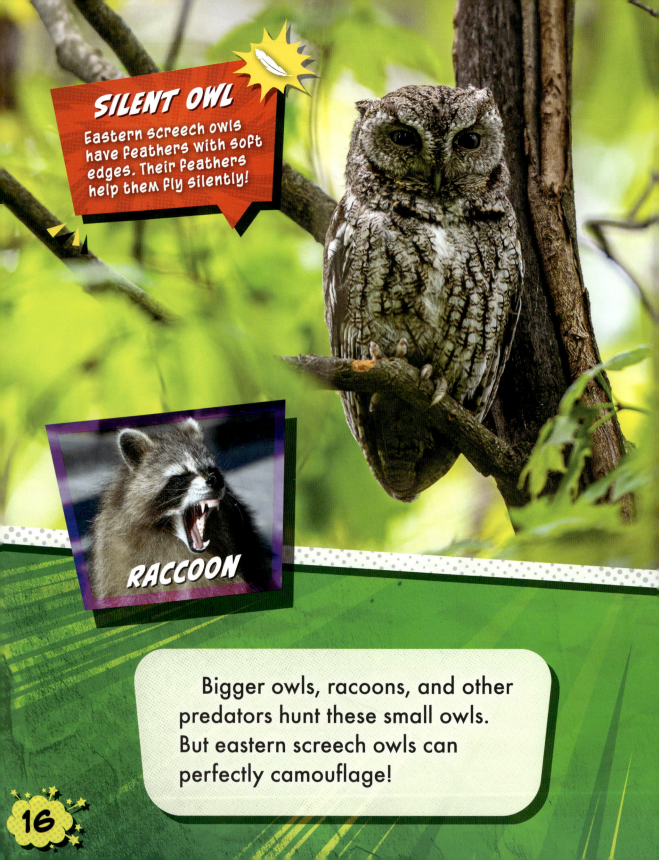

SILENT OWL
Eastern screech owls have feathers with soft edges. Their feathers help them fly silently!

RACCOON

Bigger owls, racoons, and other predators hunt these small owls. But eastern screech owls can perfectly camouflage!

FEATHERS IN ACTION!

Their grey and reddish-brown feathers blend into tree bark. They are invisible in their forest home.

HOPPING HIDERS

Arctic hares live in cold, flat areas. They may rest in **shallow** shelters. Thick fur keeps them warm.

In winter, their fur turns white. The hares blend into the snow!

ARCTIC HARE

CLASS: MAMMAL

LIFE SPAN: AROUND 3 TO 5 YEARS

STATUS IN THE WILD

| LEAST CONCERN | NEAR THREATENED | VULNERABLE | ENDANGERED | CRITICALLY ENDANGERED | EXTINCT IN THE WILD | EXTINCT |

RANGE

19

In summer, the snow melts. Arctic hares **shed** their white fur. They grow grey and brown fur to match their rocky home.

SUMMER

FUR IN ACTION!

WINTER

Invisible animals can surprise or hide. They are masters of **disguise**!

SPEED AWAY
Arctic hares are fast. They can run up to 40 miles (64 kilometers) per hour!

GLOSSARY

Arctic—related to the area around the North Pole

camouflage—to use colors and patterns to blend into surroundings

coral reefs—structures made of coral that usually grow in shallow seawater

disguise—an outward appearance that hides what something really is

invisible—unable to be seen

predators—animals that hunt other animals for food

prey—animals that are hunted by other animals for food

rain forests—thick, green forests that receive a lot of rain

shallow—not deep

shed—to lose something on the body such as fur or skin

textures—the ways something looks or feels

TO LEARN MORE

AT THE LIBRARY

Dickmann, Nancy. *Masters of Camouflage.* Tucson, Ariz.: Brown Bear Books, 2021.

Greve, Meg. *Super-camouflaged Animals.* Mankato, Minn.: Black Rabbit Books, 2025.

Romero, Libby. *Animals that Change Color.* Washington, D.C.: National Geographic Kids, 2020.

ON THE WEB

Factsurfer.com gives you a safe, fun way to find more information.

1. Go to www.factsurfer.com.

2. Enter "invisibility" into the search box and click 🔍.

3. Select your book cover to see a list of related content.

INDEX

Arctic hares, 18, 19, 20, 21
attacks, 4
Bargibant's pygmy sea horse, 7
bodies, 8, 10
camouflage, 9, 16
colors, 8, 10, 17, 19, 20
coral reefs, 8, 9
day, 15
eastern screech owls, 14, 15, 16, 17
eyes, 11
feathers, 16, 17
feathers in action, 17
fur, 18, 19, 20
fur in action, 20
hide, 4, 7, 13, 15, 21
mossy frogs, 10, 11, 12, 13
night, 12

predators, 13, 16
prey, 4, 9
pygmy sea horses, 6, 7, 8, 9
rain forests, 12
range, 7, 11, 15, 19
shed, 20
shelters, 18
size, 6, 14, 15, 16
snow, 19, 20
speed, 21
summer, 20
surprise, 4, 9, 21
tails, 9
textures, 8, 10
tree bark, 17
Vietnamese mossy frog, 11, 13
voice, 13
winter, 19

The images in this book are reproduced through the courtesy of: Thorsten Spoerlein, front cover; John, p. 3; davemhuntphoto, pp. 4, 11 (inset); Jennifer McCallum, p. 5; nickeverett1981, p. 6; Sascha Caballero, p. 7 (inset); Daniel Lamborn, p. 7 (class: fish); marwan osama, p. 8 (coral reef); John Anderson, p. 8 (inset); Mike Workman, p. 9; tonaquatic, p. 9 (prey); Thorsten Spoerlein, p. 10; shirly, p. 11 (class: amphibian); soft_light, p. 12 (rain forest); Lauren, pp. 12 (inset), 13; lavin photography, p. 14; Glass and Nature, p. 15 (inset); touchedbylight, p. 15 (class: bird); Ryan, p. 16 (raccoon); Mike, pp. 16-17; FotoRequest, p. 17 (not hidden); FotoRequest, p. 17 (hidden); Philip Mugridge/ Alamy Stock Photo, p. 18; Nick Dale, p. 19 (inset); Danielle S. Van Lier, p. 19 (class: mammal); All Canada Photos/ Alamy Stock Photo, p. 20 (summer); André Gilden/ Alamy Stock Photo, p. 20 (winter); Nick Dale/ Alamy Stock Photo, p. 21; Tony Campbell, p. 23.